Giving Your Self Away

by
Dr. Heather Ward
Wife, Mother, and Roman Catholic Parish Lay Pastoral Assistant in Nottingham

GROVE BOOKS LIMITED
Bramcote   Nottingham   NG9 3DS

CONTENTS

THE COVER PICTURE
portraying the pelican is by Terry Culkin

O loving Pelican! O Jesu Lord!
Unclean I am, but cleanse me in Thy blood!
Of which a single drop, from sinners split,
Can purge the entire world from all its guilt.
Jesu, whom for the present veil'd I see,
What I so thirst for, oh! vouchsafe to me:
That I may see Thy countenance unfolding,
And may be blest Thy glory in beholding.
                                        Amen.
(from the hymn: *O Godhead hid* by Thomas Aquinas)

First Impression August 1988
ISSN 0262-799X
ISBN 1 85174 089 9

1. BE YOURSELF?

'Be yourself' is a phrase that slips easily from the lips of ministers, Christian counsellors and, indeed, any Christian, whenever advice seems to be required. Having rejected, quite rightly, a demand for a form of self-denial which seemed to question God's wisdom in creating free and unique beings, Christians have readily embraced our culture's pre-occupation with self-image and self-affirmation. In so doing theological considerations seem to have been shelved. Few questions have been asked about the nature of the self which is to be affirmed or which previously was to be denied. Instead of articulating a theological anthropology, a vision of human personhood derived from our under-standing of God, we are in danger of installing at the heart of our pastoral work and spirituality a secular psychology with a religious veneer.

Such is my conclusion from the experience of leading seminars on the subject of selfhood, for clergy and laity, Anglican and Roman Catholic. I would argue that the development (or rather, renewal) of theological anthropology is an urgent need of the churches. Our vision of selfhood, that is, of the primal identity of the human being, has consequences not only for Christian formation, pastoral care and spirituality, but also for our approach to liturgy, community and social theology.

In Christian formation the present tendency is to concentrate on the 'faith-story' of the individual. But this story is of little consequence long-term unless the story-teller is offered an understanding of who this experienc-ing 'I' is and how (s)he is related to God whose name is 'I AM'. Coming to faith involves a new understanding of our personal identity as issuing from, and hidden in, God, the source of all life, who alone can say 'I AM' without reference to any other, and in whom 'we live and move and have our being' (Acts 17.26, 28).

It involves, furthermore, glimpsing that this very notion of personal exist-ence involves relationship, both with God and with other persons. The dis-covery begins to be made that the acceptance of derivation and relationship are integral to the idea of identity. Being made in the image of God we cannot say 'I' independently of him. We must acknowledge our-selves as created and dependent. But this God whose name is 'I AM' also reveals himself to us as a Trinity, as a communion of persons. We must recognize that our own derived 'I-ness' is similarly a capacity for being-in-relationship as the image of his. Our acceptance of Christ as redeemer issues from this first apprehension of relationship, of a relationship which is broken and beyond our power to restore.

Our faith-story, our understanding of the continuing process of conver-sion and sanctification in our lives, needs to be set within the context of God's purpose in creation and redemption to fashion and restore not individuals, but a people, a race, a community of persons: this F. D. Maurice discerned in his commentaries on the Gospel of St. John:
    'I do not want a separate life either here or hereafter. I come to
    renounce that separate life, to disclaim it, to say what a wretch I am

for pretending to have it, for trying to create it . . . I understand that the Son of God, by sacrificing himself, has given me a share and a property in another life—the common life, the universal life which is in him.'[1]

In much of our pastoral care and spiritual direction the proper concern with the affirmation of our humanity as God's gift has gradually developed into an equation of personal, psychological growth with holiness. Classical 'care of souls' has always focussed attention away from the psychology and experiences of an individual towards God. A great director like St. Francis de Sales was intent upon hiding the person from herself in a 'holy indifference' to assessments of development and maturity.[2] Growth, understood as increasing likeness to God, was not to be feverishly sought for its own sake but patiently awaited as a gift from God, while centering total effort on a simple being-for-God in every aspect of life, an approach exemplified by his counsel

'Trees only bear fruit in the presence of the sun. Let us dwell in the presence of God, which will help us, sooner or later, to bear fruit.'[3]

To such spiritual guides as St. Francis 'wholeness is holiness' could only mean that holiness consists in being wholly for God, whole-hearted, whole-willed in the quest for God. 'Wholeness' refers simply to the nature of the person's relationship with God, referring the person beyond themselves towards God.

Increasingly today we witness a shift towards wholeness as the perfecting of personality, so that holiness becomes synonymous with psychological maturity, and growth is identified with the resolution of personality problems. The focus remains inwards upon the individuality of the person and the furtherance of their attributes. Nurture in such an atmosphere of self-cultivation as the supreme value does not prepare the contemporary Christian to respond to the call for radical self-dispossession which the New Testament presents as God's way to become human (see Phil. 2.5-7). Spiritual direction needs to recover the approach to human wholeness delineated by Aelred Squire:

'. . . redeemed man, in common with every man of good will, will have to do a good deal of hard thinking about what human wholeness is, and even make a great deal of positive effort to achieve that wholeness. But he will also, in practice, constantly have to give that wholeness up and, apparently die to it too, because his true centre lies in being *at all costs* open to relationship with the One who is so eternally and abundantly alive that he can snatch life out of death. Man finds his life ultimately by losing it. This is the distinguishing mark of the Christian Way.'[4]

[1] Frederick Denison Maurice, *The Gospel of St. John—a series of discourses* (Macmillan, London, 1878), p.113.
[2] See discussion in *St. Francis de Sales and the Order of the Visitation* (Monastery of the Visitation, Waldron, 1962), pp.9-10.
[3] Claude Roffat *Everyone must pray* (Selected texts of St. Francis de Sales) (S. F. S. Publications, Bangalore, 1982), p.14.
[4] Aelred Squire, *Asking the Fathers* (S.P.C.K., London, 1973) p.34.

Our approach to liturgy, community and social theology suffers equally from our loss of anthropology. The requirement of sharing, participation, 'togetherness' etc., conceived of only in terms of speech, activity, extroversion, lacks theological foundations. It views all human activity only from the perspective of the social psychologist, concentrating upon behavioural manifestations. A theological base for our pastoral strategies demands a grasp of ontology and of the ontological bonds between human beings. Similarly, it is easy for many social comments and actions to be dismissed as 'political' because we have not established sufficiently the theological basis for our convictions about human dignity, human rights, social responsibility.

In every major area of church life we find a need for a clear conceptual and linguistic framework within which we can operate. I would suggest that the vision of selfhood developed by the patristic and monastic/mystical tradition may still provide just such a framework.

2. MAN NOT MEN

Often today we find it difficult to talk in terms of 'Man' or 'humanity': developments in philosophy, psychology and sociology have called into question any idea of an unchanging human nature. Theologically we look in both directions. From Nominalism we inherit an extreme emphasis on the individuality of all existing things and the impossibility of one being participating in another. From Descartes we have acquired an emphasis on selfhood as individual consciousness and rationality: 'I think therefore I am.' Both legacies encourage us to think in terms of individuals, men, women, rather than of Man; to use the term 'personal' synonymously with 'individual'. Yet any presentation of doctrine maintains some vision of a consistent inner identity uniting humankind, a possibility of speaking with meaning of 'human nature'. The point is, of course, that this second usage is neither psychological nor philosophical: it considers Man as a spiritual being. We are concerned with the spiritual identity of the human person, rather than with individuals' differing psychological attributes.

The failure to make this crucial distinction between the psychological and the spiritual bedevils all our attempts to understand in Christian terms that injunction 'be yourself'. As Philip Sherrard has pointed out, the development of Christian thought in the West has produced a conflation of 'pneuma', spirit, with 'psyche', soul, mind or personality.[1] We rarely speak of a person as a spirit-soul-and-body entity, but as a body-soul, body-mind entity. 'Soul' has to denote both spiritual and psychological attributes and easily equates, in philosophical and common parlance, with mind or self. The result may be either to equate mind with brain, reducing self-as-soul to an epiphenomenon of brain, or to sacralize our psycho-physical attributes as the self which must be fulfilled.

The patristic frame of reference, in contrast, maintains the Pauline concept of man as body, soul and spirit, the spirit giving that likeness to God which is at the centre of the account of creation in Genesis. Man's psycho-physical properties derive from the dust of the earth, but it is the spirit, the breath of God within him, which makes him, a living being, which makes him 'Man'. And so, when St. Irenaeus wrote 'The glory of God is a living man'[2], it is Man as this spiritual being, fully reflecting the image and likeness of God to whom he refers. It is Man as a unique representative of Manhood, of human identity, who *is* the 'glory', the effulgence of the Creator, not the individual who reflects only his psycho-physical attributes, however well-developed. For Irenaeus, to be fully a person,

[1] Philip Sherrard, 'The Christian Understanding of Man' in *Sobornost* 7, 5 (1977) pp.329-342. Sherrard sees the conflation as beginning with the rise of Western Nominalism. My own examination of late medieval literary texts supports this view, although the full conflation of mind and soul occurs from the time of the Age of Enlightenment.

[2] H. Bettenson, *The Early Fathers of the Church* (O.U.P., London, 1956) p.104. I have used this helpful anthology for its clear translation, while referring to Irenaeus of Lyons *Five books against the heresies* (trans. John Keble) (J. & H. Parker, Oxford, Library of Fathers of the Holy Catholic Church, 1872).

St Irenaeus of Lyons (C130-200) brought up in Asia Minor. His main defence concern was the defence of Catholic tradition V Gnosticism long treatise v the Heresies. 1st Christian write to make the explicit po. that the purpose of God's sharing of human life is that we may share divine life.

fully Man, fully human, is to be 'pneumatic', that is, spiritual: 'carnal' Man, the human being living only as a body-soul entity, is not yet a self:

'There are three elements of which . . . the complete man is made up, flesh, soul and spirit: one of these preserves and fashions the man, and this is spirit; another is given unity and form by the first, and this is flesh; the third, the soul, is mid-way between the two, and sometimes it is subservient to the spirit and is raised by it; while sometimes it allies itself with flesh and descends to earthly passions . . .

'When this spirit is mingled with soul and united with created matter, then through the outpouring of the Spirit, the complete man is produced: this is man in the image of God. A man with soul only, lacking spirit, is "psychic": such a man is carnal, unfinished, incomplete.'[1]

To become a self is to actualize our *spiritual* nature, opening it up to God and thereby bringing our psycho-physical being into harmony with him. A self, therefore, is a perfected human image of God, who reflects the whole nature of man within his own particularized identity: he may truly be called 'another Christ' by grace, for he reflects the nature of Christ who took on the whole of human nature in the Incarnation and who is as Man fully 'pneumatic'.

We must not, however, reify selfhood. St. Irenaeus thinks of the self as basically a capacity for receiving and responding to God, rather than as a pre-existent entity. It is 'through the outpouring of the (Holy) Spirit' being received by the human spirit that the 'complete man' is made. The essence of our selfhood resides in our capacity for continuing acceptance of the gift of God's life-giving Spirit: the receptiveness of our spirit to the Holy Spirit then allows the activation of all the gifts we have from God by nature; that is, our specific psychological and physical attributes.

Following accepted usage we may call Irenaeus' carnal Manhood 'ego'. 'Ego' thus refers to all that Man is as an animal, and to his self-definition and self-image, the products of psychic consciousness. 'Self' is then retained for the spiritual Man, who is not dominated by ego but stands free from it, acknowledging that this ego is neither his source nor his identity.

The self, as integrated spirit-soul-body, should be conceived of as inclusive of ego. However, as we see from the passage of St. Irenaeus, the psyche, our personality, may ally with our instinctual nature in ways which deny the primacy of spirit. Ego may conflict with spirit. Consequently, in our discussion 'self', although implicitly inclusive of ego, will be used to denote spiritual identity as it stands over against the pretensions of the ego. Ego, when used specifically in opposition to self, will denote the personality regarded as the centre and purpose of its own existence. Self looks outwards to God, in acceptance of life and human attributes as gift. Ego looks inwards upon itself as the source and sustainer of its own gifts.

[1] *Ibid.,* p.97.

We are created to share — soul & body — in God's light & glory.

The defeat of ego by the self, therefore, is not the destruction of personality but its dethronement from its dominant, spirit-suppressing centrality and its re-instatement under the influence of spirit, which orientates
it rightly towards God.[1]

Approached within this conceptual framework 'becoming oneself' is synonymous with repentance, for repentance is the process of turning
towards God in which the movement is best understood, as Thomas Merton has said, as a turning of oneself inside-out.[2] Ego-dominated Man is
Man turned in on himself, against his nature as a being made to receive his
existence from beyond himself. To become his spiritual self he must continually turn his inner being outwards towards God, its rightful state, an
experience of warfare with ego which feels like a putting to death of all
that is understood as himself.

This vision of selfhood differs in one other radical way from our current
psychological model. The tendency to focus on personality has resulted in
an inability to recognize the spiritual relationship between one person and
another. If there is no unifying concept of humanity, that is, of person-
hood, to which we can refer, then the only bonds we can discern between
people are those we create. We find ourselves obliged to *create*
fellowship; we experience and perceive putting ourselves aside for others
as an imperative imposed on us solely by the necessities of social life or
Commandment. We do not understand it as emerging from within our
own spiritual nature.

Starting from the premise of spiritual selfhood produces an altogether dif-
ferent approach to human relationship from that offered by psychology.
The patristic understanding of Man holds him to be at once unique and
encompassing of all humanity, as we have seen, just as the Persons of the
Trinity are each entirely God and entirely distinctive. Hence each person,
uniquely called by his own name, yet stands for, stands on behalf of, all
other people. This means that the self is in essence a related and relating
being, and, moreover, a vicarious being. Not only relationship but also
intercession is found to be constitutive of the self, so that intercession
must be understood as a state to be lived-out rather than as an optional
activity to be performed. The self is therefore never an isolated entity,
making its quite separate way in life and towards God, nor yet is it simply
part of an organism or collective, lacking individuation.

The novelist Charles Dickens understood this well when he portrayed
Esther Summerson in *Bleak House.* In the crisis of a fever Esther sees a
luminous ring of beads of which she is one, and the pain of living is such
that she begs to be taken off it. Esther's illness is contracted because she
alone has cared for an unwanted street-sweeper with typhus-fever. Her
suffering results from her simple recognition of mutual responsibility. Her
pain links her with the pain of all humanity. Like the bead which echoes
the shape of the whole ring and of every other bead, while having its own

[1] See, for example, A. L. Clements *The mystical poetry of Thomas Traherne* (Harvard Univer-
sity Press, Cambridge, Mass., 1969).
[2] Thomas Merton, *The Climate of Monastic Prayer* (Cistercian Publications, Shannon,
1969) p.147.

place on the circle, Esther understands her relationship to the totality of mankind and to each one. Her living as a full self exposes her to innocent suffering, to experiencing painfully that she is 'bonded in being'.

This approach to the self overcomes our contemporary tendency to perceive spirituality as separate from social involvement and therefore as requiring an external yoking. It becomes clear that we cannot talk about the self in isolation. Consideration of the nature of the person automatically produces a consideration of his relationship to his fellow persons. Consideration of our creation as images of a God who is Trinity likewise necessitates consideration of that self in the wider social world, as Kallistos Ware asserts:

> 'Made after the image of God the Trinity, human beings are called to reproduce on earth the mystery of mutual love that the Trinity lives in Heaven . . . Each social unit—the family, the school, the workshop, the parish, the Church universal—is to be made an ikon of the Trinity. Because we know that God is three in one, each of us is committed to living sacrificially in and for the other; each is committed irrevocably to a life of practical service, of active compassion.'[1]

The 'Family of Man' thus becomes not a cant, worn-out political phrase but a theological truth, providing the basis of our ethical and social teaching.

---

[1] Kallistos Ware, *The Orthodox Way* (Mowbray, London, 1979) p.49.

3. EGO-DENIAL AND SELF-DENIAL—THE MYSTICAL TRADITION

If we embrace this concept of selfhood it becomes clear that the Christian has two inter-related tasks: to fulfil his pneumatic self, bringing his ego under the direction of self, and to repudiate the usurpation of this self-hood by ego. In other words to 'be yourself' necessitates not 'self-denial' but 'ego-denial'. To become the full image of God we must reject that false image of ourselves which puts our personality, needs, abilities, at the centre of our existence. The ego has a constant inclination towards being a 'self-made man'; it is ego which asserts itself as independent of God and others, setting its rights, needs and instincts over against them. It is ego which believes that existence, love, acceptance, redemption, are earned by the merits and qualities of our personality. Ego rejects the notion of all life and salvation as free gifts, turning the person away from his true life-source. And so, as for Milton's Satan in *Paradise Lost*, devotion to ego is devotion to death.

This is the Christian understanding of Jesus' words about losing one's life to gain it. We must abandon our own understanding of ourselves, all that we mean by ego, so that his life may grow in us making us 'sons in the Son', images of the perfect image of the Father. Such ego-denial is there-fore not negative but positive: it is the sacrifice only of all that prevents our having life in abundance.

This vision of selfhood in opposition to egotism is frequently found in mystical writings, giving rise to unfounded accusations of self-obsession, on the one hand, and rejection of humanity, on the other. Superficially St. Catherine of Genoa's famous saying 'My me is God nor do I recognize any other me, except God himself'[1] is either heretical substance-mysticism (the belief that man is the same being as God by nature) or gross self-aggrandisement. Heard in the knowledge of pneumatic selfhood it appears otherwise.

Catherine's *Dialogue* operates within the same framework as that of St. Irenaeus. Spirit is set against natural Man, self against ego. Catherine refuses to identify her being with natural Man, affirming that it is through spirit that she is brought into communion with God, source of life. Her capacity to say 'I am' derives not from the qualities of her natural, psychic existence but from her creation in the image of God whose name is 'I AM'. Catherine's life of extreme asceticism was aimed not at destroying her unique identity but at controlling all that impeded that identity.

St. Catherine taught and lived a way of complete detachment from her ego, accepting her life minute by minute as a gift from God. A similar vision is found in St. John of the Cross, whose teaching on detachment

[1] Baron F. Von Hugel, *The Mystical Element in Religion* (2 vols.) (J. M. Dent, London, 1908) Vol. 1, p.265.

10

has often been rejected as cold and inhuman. St. John was concerned that those under his direction should attain to 'transforming union' which is the fullness of selfhood: Man is made for a union with God which makes him also his image. Attainment of this full humanity requires the person to be free from the delusion of being an independent, possessing entity. He must be empty of all pretensions to be or have anything as by right, free to receive all as gift. So we must read the starkness of his famous lines from *The Ascent of Mount Carmel*

'To arrive at possessing all, desire to possess nothing
To arrive at being all, desire to be nothing,'[1]

in the light of his vision of the plenitude awaiting the self:

'Mine are the heavens and mine is the earth,
Mine are the nations, the just are mine and mine are the sinners.
'The angels are mine and the Mother of God and all things are mine;
and God himself is mine and for me,
because Christ is mine and all for me.
What do you ask then and seek, my soul?
Yours is all this and all is for you.
Do not engage in something less,
nor pay heed to the crumbs which fall from your Father's table.
Go forth and exult in your glory!'[2]

While we hold on to our ego, regarding it as the sum-total of our identity, and seek its fulfilment, we cannot reach the full dimensions of our humanity. To choose ego is the truly destructive act of self-denial.

Parallel apparent contradictions are also found in the writings of the Cambridge Platonists, those seventeenth century scholars whose thought has had a profound effect on English religious thought. In the work of Benjamin Whichcote we find, for example, the assertion that 'It is the chiefest of Good Things for a man to be himself.'[3] Remarkably modern it seems, until further reading reveals a vision of that man as one who has 'universalized himself.'[4] The self in question is not the restricted, psychic ego, but the spiritual being who encompasses the whole of humanity and is 'a candle of the Lord', a small, created reflection of the Lord of Light.

Remarkably close to St. John of the Cross is John Smith's comment on the truly poor man who will

'triumph in nothing more than his own Nothing-ness and in the All-ness of the Divinity. But indeed this his being Nothing is the only way to be all things, this his having nothing the truest way of possessing all things.'[5]

As soon as we lay claim to ourselves, identifying ourselves with our ego, we limit what we are able to receive from God. Where ego predominates God-given identity is squeezed out.

[1] 'The Ascent of Mount Carmel' in *The Complete Works of St. John of the Cross* (trans. and ed. Otilio Rodriguez, and Keiran Kavanaugh), (Institute of Carmelite Studies, Washington, 1976) p.103.
[2] 'Prayer of a soul enkindled with love' in *ibid.*, p.613.
[3] Benjamin Whichcote Aphorisms in W. C. de Pauley, *The Candle of the Lord* (Books for Libraries Press, Freeport, 1937) p.69.
[4] *Ibid.*, p.15.
[5] John Smith 'The excellency and nobleness of true religion' in *ibid.*, p.191.

The claim of idependence and distinctiveness for the ego is, as we have seen, illusory. Psychic, 'natural' man derives his qualities from the common genetic pool. He has no responsibility for them and, rather than distinguishing him, they link him with the rest of men. To believe in one's *natural* identity as the source of our uniqueness is self-delusion. William Law, the Anglican non-juror and mystical writer, was a perceptive analyst of this delusion. He presented the conflict between self and ego as that between an 'inner Cain' and an 'inner Abel':

> 'You are under the power of no other enemy, are held in no other captivity and want no other deliverance but from the power of your own earthly self. This is the murderer of the divine life within you. It is your own Cain that murders your own Abel.'[1]

Why Cain? It is Cain who breaks the bonds linking him to God and to mankind, in his killing of Abel. Cain seeks an independence of God and of his brother and is therefore an ideal exemplar of the ego which asserts itself as a 'self-made man.'

Law's use of the Cain-Abel antithesis directs our attention to another vital aspect of this vision of selfhood. We have seen so far that pneumatic selfhood is equated with Christ-like selfhood because Christ is the perfect image of the Father. Left like this Christ could be seen simply as an example, a model for man. This tradition of thought and experience goes far beyond this. It does, indeed, see Christ as the 'pattern' for our selfhood, but not as an externally applied one, to be simply copied by us. Rather, Christ is, as it were, the basic carbon, or the spiritual 'genetic' pattern, of all human selfhood. When we become what we are, we find ourselves like him, conformed to him from the inside, as St. John's First Epistle says:

> 'it does not yet appear what we shall be, but we know that when he appears we shall be like him, for we shall see him as he is. And everyone who thus hopes in him purifies himself as he is pure.' (1 John 3.2-3)

The eschatological tension of 'the already and the not yet' is present within the self: created in the image of God the person has yet to fulfill that likeness to him. The process of becoming what we are in him is, therefore, inevitably, as St. John indicates, one of purification, of shedding all that distorts the growth into that image. And just as the chemical process of purification by distillation produces a change of state and an apparent disintegration, so too the process of spiritual purification will be experienced as an 'un-doing', as a painful change of state, as a breaking-up of a settled mode of being and of interpreting that being. To come to the truth of one's self as Abel-Christ requires confrontation with Cain whom we have embraced as our identity. Again self-fulfilment is synonymous with repentance. In imitating Christ and denying our ego we become full persons: this is one aspect of 'denial' or 'sacrifice' in Christian experience.

But Christ, our inner pattern, *is* typified by Abel, the innocent, righteous victim, the subject of sacrifice; and Christ is also the Lamb of God, the

[1] William Law, 'The Spirit of Love' in *A Serious Call to a Devout and Holy life. The Spirit of Love* (ed. Paul Stanwood), (S.P.C.K., London, 1975) p.375 and see 1 John 3, 11-12.

Lamb of Sacrifice. We reach the paradox that when the Christian glimpses, through his efforts at ego-denial, the selfhood that is his, he finds it is still characterized by another kind of renunciation, God's own self-dispossession in the Incarnation and the Cross.

The other motivation towards the state of 'being nothing and having nothing' in all Christian mystics is the longing to be as the Beloved has been in his human experience. Implicit within this is the recognition of a connection between God and the idea of sacrifice. This recognition was made explicit by the Anglican theologians F. D. Maurice and George Mac-Donald in the nineteenth century.

4. THE SELF THAT GIVES ITSELF AWAY—INSIGHTS FROM THE VICTORIAN AGE

The concept of the self as the image of God in man was essential to the thinking of F. D. Maurice, who is best known, perhaps, for his inception of Christian Socialism. Maurice approached the human person through his understanding of Christ. For Maurice, Christ is pre-eminently the Son of the Father and thereby Elder Brother of the human race. This sonship and brotherhood belongs to Christ by nature, they define him; if, therefore, man is made to the likeness of Christ, sonship and brotherhood belong equally to his essence: for Maurice there was no speaking of the human person in terms other than those of such relationships. To be a self is to acknowledge oneself as a related, relating, and derived being, speaking ontologically and not psychologically. Socially it is possible to be orphaned, ontologically never. Hence for Maurice the renunciation of the claim to be an isolated individual, king of one's own castle, was 'simply a person confessing to be what he is.'[1] In all this we see, of course, his agreement with the earliest Christian vision of the self.

In his study of Job Maurice perceived Man in Luther's terms as at once a sinner and justified; Job is aware of the entrapment within ego which is his 'great prison-house', and of his relationship with God which brings him intimations of a goodness within him, coming from God and not from himself. Man is caught in the tension between his nature as a creature made from the dust of the earth and tending back to it and his nature as a spiritual being destined for glory by virtue of God's grace. All Maurice's claims for the greatness of the self as child and brother or sister were made within the context of this tension, as shown in his letter to a friend:

> 'Hope—hope that I, the meanest of God's creatures, for such to myself I must appear, am destined for the noblest purposes and the highest glory—is that which alone can make me humble and keep me so . . .

> 'You must aspire high if you would know yourself to be nothing. If you would feel yourself to be the worm that you are you must claim your privilege of being like God.'[2]

The centrality of God in Maurice's thinking about humanity led him beyond the concept of ego-denial in his understanding of the relationship between sacrifice and selfhood. His study of the Old Testament led him to see God as essentially self-renouncing, so that sacrifice belonged to his nature. In considering the renunciations asked of Abraham he concluded that

> 'Abraham found sacrifice to be no one solitary act, no sudden expression of joy, no violent effort to make a return for blessings which we can only return by accepting; but that it was at the very root of our being; that our lives stand upon it; that society is held together by it;

[1] Quoted in Frank M. MacClain, *Maurice: Man and Moralist* (S.P.C.K., London, 1967) p.73.
[2] 'Letter to Acland' in Frederick Maurice (ed.) *The life of F. D. Maurice, chiefly told in his own letters* (2 vols., Macmillan, London, 1884), 1, 143.

that all power to be right or to do right begins with the offering up of ourselves, because it is thus that the righteous Lord makes us like himself.'[1]

Consequently, on turning to the New Testament Maurice saw in Christ's Cross the fullest revelation of God's nature: Christ is fully 'the Lamb slain before the foundation of the world' (Rev. 13.8). The Cross is not a reaction wrung from God by man's sin but God being himself, totally abandoned for the life of his children. Contrary to some modern thinking, the Cross is not God's bringing of good out of failure but the ultimate expression of a divine self-hood which must 'pour itself out' (Phil. 2.7) in order to be itself.

If, then, sacrifice belongs to God, it must also belong to Man as God's image. Sacrifice is the means whereby 'the righteous Lord makes us like himself', fulfilling his image in us, but the perfected image will in turn reflect the self-dispossession of God. Sacrifice is both the means of attaining selfhood and its fulfilment. To be a self, ego must be denied, but the self so liberated will be one which is continually abandoning itself. The self must be ever in the process of relinquishing its claims, its possessions, its sense of an established identity, living for and on behalf of others.

These themes come together in the works of George MacDonald, whose fame as the inspiration of C. S. Lewis's fantasy-stories has over-shadowed his own achievement. His works are focussed on Christian life as the actualization of divinely-given selfhood as divine sonship, the discovery of our being in and from *the* Being:

> 'Thou art the only person,
> and I cry
> Unto the father of this
> my 1.'[2]

and on the temptation to deny this derivation and dependence, establishing ourselves according to our own choices:

> 'Shall I be born of God
> or of mere man?
> Be made like Christ, or
> on some other plan?'[3]

He sets before us the option of 'god-ness' or 'self-ness', co-operation with God in the fulfilment of his image in us, or the creation of an idol, our ego, in an image of our own devising.

MacDonald's approach jealously guards the uniqueness of the self. Like the persons of the Trinity each person is a distinctiveness-in-unity. Man's

[1] F. D. Maurice, *The Doctrine of Sacrifice deduced from the Scriptures* (Macmillan, London, 1893) p.91. Useful on this subject are Michael Ramsey's discussion of the Biblical basis for Maurice's position and the discussion of Dame Frideswide Sandemann of Philippians 2, 2-5, which endorse this vision of sacrifice in God: see A. M. Ramsey, *The Christian Concept of Sacrifice* (S.L.G. Press, Oxford, 1974) see also Dame Frideswide Sandemann, 'Some Aspects of Modern Spirituality and the Rule of St. Benedict' in *Cistercian Studies* 15,2 (1980) 208.

[2] George MacDonald, *A Book of Strife, in the Form of a Diary of an Old Soul* (London, 1882), p.165.

[3] *Ibid.,* p.41.

divine sonship identifies the self as brother to every other self, without confusion of identities. True to the pattern of Christ's nature, Man the brother (or sister) is vicarious, living for, and on behalf of, all other selves, while retaining particularity. But this particularity is safeguarded by God, not by the person, whose task is co-operation in the salvation of his brothers. The self cannot conceive of union with God apart from union with his brothers, as seen in his novel *Robert Falconer,* when his title character considers the damned:

> 'Noo we hae nae merit, an they hae nae merit, an' what for are we here and they there? But we're washed clean and innocent noo; and noo, whar ther's no wyte lying upon ousel's, it seems to me that we micht beir some o' the sins o' them 'at hae ower many. I call upo' ilk ane ye 'at has fren' or neebor down yonner, to rise up an' taste nor bite nor sup mair till we gang up a' thegither to the fut o' the throne, an' pray the Lord to lat's gang and due as the Maister did afore's an' beir their griefs an' carry their sorrows doon in hell there; gin it may be tha they may repent an' get remission o' their sins an' come up here wi' us at the long last.'[1]

St. Paul's readiness to be condemned for the sake of his fellow-Jews (Romans 9.3) is understood as the paradigm of true selfhood.

Since the uniqueness of the self is safe in God, being, as an image of Christ, God's secret (Col. 2.2) revealed only when we see him as he is (1 John 3.2-3), it cannot be discovered by searching for it. It can only be realized by removing the obstacles to union of our will with the will of God, its keeper: that is, by ego-denial.

Furthermore, since the self is hidden in God, it follows that the self on earth, separated from God, is never complete. The self must grow towards God in this life, grow into its identity, not by seeking experiences but by seeking to unite our will-to-life with God's will:

> 'Thou hast me, statue-like, hewn in the rough,
> Meaning at last to shape me perfectly,
> Lord, thou hast called me forth,
> I turn and call on thee . . .

> 'The life that hath not willed itself to be
> Must clasp the life that willed and be at peace:
> Or, like a leaf, wind-blown, through chaos flee;
> A life husk into which the demons go, . . .

> 'But when I turn and grasp the making hand
> And will the making will, with confidence
> I ride the crest of the creation-wave,
> Helpless no more, no more existence's slave;
> In the heart of love's creating fire I stand,
> And, love-possessed in heart and soul and sense,
> Take up the making share the making Master gave.'[2]

[1] George MacDonald, *Robert Falconer* (Hurst and Blackett, London, n.d.) p.82.
[2] *Book of Strife, op. cit.,* p.83.

Seeking union with God the Creator brings true creativity to the self, a participation in the creativity and fruitfulness of God.

Macdonald's self is, thus, the repenting self, the self that exists 'in God' but must enter into the process of actualization through renunciation of ego. But the self that is gradually being freed into life in God is not thereby freed from the necessity of sacrifice, because God's liberty is seen as a liberty to abandon himself to others. MacDonald's God is not a well but a fountain of life; a God who is characterized by ecstasy, that is, by a going beyond the boundaries of self, as a character in his novel *Wilfred Cumbermede* asserts:

> 'if ever there were such a thing as a self always giving itself away, that self would be God.'[1]

So when, through ego-abandonment, the person becomes what he is, he finds himself the image of a self-abandoning God. The human self, too, must be imaged forth not as well but as a fountain springing up to eternal life (John 4.14)

---

[1] George MacDonald, *Wilfred Cumbermede* (Kegan Paul, Trench and Trubner, London, n.d.) p.308.

5. WHEN GOD COMES TO A MAN, MAN LOOKS FOR A NEIGHBOUR[1]

That there are social dimensions to this vision of selfhood is evident. Maurice and his associates in the Christian Socialist movement, such as Charles Kingsley, were inspired purely by their theology. They saw in the rise of an industrialized and capitalist society the creation of a social system destructive of man's very nature. If people are by nature and grace brother and sister, ontologically bound to one another, then social structures must honour and reflect this reality. A society in which the only bonds recognized between persons were those of the 'cash-nexus'— employer and employee, buyer and seller—and which rested upon competition, was held to be going against the grain of creation:

> 'to pretend that any society can ever be founded upon competition is about as fearful a mockery as to say that a tortured wretch rests upon the stake that impales him.'[2]

Like Thomas Carlyle, who had linked his contemporaries to Cain as murderers of their brother[3], these early Christian Socialists understood the social developments of their age, which set man against man as solitary individuals, as a large-scale manifestation of ego. The new social system, as Carlyle claimed, instituted the 'new sacrament of divorce', men denying all relationship to, and derivation from, God and their fellows, and consequently refusing to bear one another's burdens.[4] The Christian Socialist movement based its pleas for co-operation and for recognition of the workers' human dignity *as* workers upon their vision of the divine origin and destiny of Man known through Christ the Elder Brother. In the following extract from a suggested sermon on the eucharist Maurice's appeal for the recognition of the value of the little regarded labourer arises solely from his theology:

> 'Has it struck you that we are not merely the countrymen of Bacon, Shakespeare and Milton, but also of some millions of men, living on our own soil, and in our own day, speaking our own tongue, who work with their hands and who have besides these hands senses which converse with this earth, sympathies that should unite them each to each, spirits that converse with God ... you can, *if you will,* say to them, one and all, *"Brothers, here are the pledges that you have a great Elder Brother".'*[5]

The eucharist is indeed for Maurice the 'sacrament of unity', opposing the 'sacrament of divorce' being newly established in his society.

Similarly Maurice's associate, Charles Kingsley, advocated the rights of the working man as the rights of brothers under the Fatherhood of God. In

---

[1] George MacDonald, *Annals of a Quiet Neighbourhood,* (Hurst and Blackett, London, 1867) p.173.
[2] *Tracts on Christian Socialism* (Christian Social Union, London, 1888) Tract 6, p.11.
[3] Thomas Carlyle, 'Past and Present', in *Collected works of Thomas Carlyle* (ed. H. D. Traill) (Chapman and Hall, London, 1898) p.149. Here Carlyle tells the story of the Irish widow, dying of typhus-fever on the street because no-one would accept responsibility for her:
> 'Behold I am sinking bare of help; Ye must help me. I am your sister, bone of your bone, one God made us, ye must help me! They answer "No, impossible; thou art no sister of ours." But she proves this sisterhood; her typhus-fever kills them: they actually were her brothers, though denying it'.
[4] *Latter-Day Pamphlets, ibid.,* p.25.
[5] F. D. Maurice, *Theological essays* (Macmillan, 1871) p.60.

Alton Locke he urged his readers to look to God's relationship with humanity as the source of their political actions:

'You are free; God has made you free. You are equals—you are brothers, for he is your King, who is no respecter of persons. He is your king, to whom all power is given in heaven and earth; who reigns and will reign, till he has put all enemies under his feet. That was Luther's charter. That is your charter and mine; the everlasting ground of our rights, our mights, our duties . . . Own no other. Claim your investiture as free men from none but God.'[1]

Kingsley feared that the 'charter' of the Chartist Movement was based upon the same individualist vision of life which caused the labourer's woes. The first requisite for the worker was not to bind himself to other workers as an individual yoking with others against an alien enemy but to reclaim the bonds of his sonship and brotherhood and then to awaken a similar recognition in his employer. The vision is truly of the collaboration—the working together—of persons in a society rather than of the secular Socialist's class struggle.

Their understanding of selfhood guided Maurice and his associates towards a new perspective on the family in society. They approached the family as a potential icon of the divine reality of human brotherhood, sisterhood and 'child-ship' which was constantly being made into an idol by the ego, representing, as it were, ego-writ-large. Human bonds which were intended to reflect divine realities and to direct the person towards apprehension of 'bonding-in-being' were being misinterpreted as exclusive relationships. Derivation and dependence were admitted only within the closed family circle. Like the ego, the family could turn in upon itself, as its own creator and sustainer, rather than outwards towards God and others. For Maurice the task of the parent was to initiate children into awareness that

'the Absolute and Eternal God has taken them to His own children, the members of Christ, the inheritors of the Kingdom of Heaven.'[2]

True parents point their offspring beyond themselves to the origin of all parenthood and beyond their siblings to their brothers and sisters in God, as MacDonald avers:

'Why does my brother come of the same mother and father? Why do I behold the helplessness of his infancy? I have had the sons of my mother that I may learn the universal brotherhood. For there is a bond between me and the most wretched liar that ever died for the murder he would not confess, closer infinitely than that which springs only from having one mother and father. That we are the sons and daughters of God . . . is a bond closer than all other bonds in one.'[3]

Like the selves within the family, the family unit must continually give itself away, renouncing its own attachment to family ties in response to the needs of the larger family. Maurice and MacDonald valued the family as the basic element in society because it was this potential icon and 'school of the Lord's service.' They deprecated any lesser vision of the family as a strong, self-contained and isolated 'brick' in the social fabric.

---

[1] Charles Kingsley, *Alton Locke* (Macmillan, London, 1895) p.435.
[2] F. D. Maurice, *What is Revelation?* (Macmillan, Cambridge, 1859) p.390.
[3] George MacDonald, *Unspoken Sermons* (Dalby, Isbister and Co., London 1876) p.206.

6. 'MY ME IS GOD'—IMPLICATIONS FOR TODAY

This concept of the self has, as I have suggested, consequences in every sphere of Christian activity. Pastorally, it enables us to discern more clearly the end of our 'care of souls.' It does not remove the difficulties inherent in counselling those who are depressed, hopeless or in rebellion against the demands of relationship or society. It does, however, provide a vision of human life and potential against which we can set the tensions, confusions and guilt of human experience. It offers a guideline when confronted by the person oppressed by the rampant ego of another or the person making a unilateral declaration of independence in response to pain. It enables us to distinguish between acknowledging the usefulness of the methods and insights of modern humanistic psychology and acceptance of the tendency towards ego-centred individualism of its world-view. It will ensure that we understand this psychology *as* psychology, as an approach to the problems of personality, and not as an anthropology offering a full vision of Man.

In our teaching and nurturing of spiritual life a grasp of this concept will ensure that it is grounded in our doctrine of God, for, as Fr. Lev Gillet has said,

'The basis of spiritual life is not psychological but ontological. Therefore an accurate treatise on spirituality is not the description of certain states of soul . . . but the objective application of definite theological principles to the individual soul.'[1]

It will therefore provide an analytical tool for evaluating current developments in the field of spirituality, making available to us Maurice's distinction between 'subjective' and 'personal' religion. 'Subjective' religion centres the person upon experiences, states of mind, feelings, in order to discover identity and relationship to God: it is focussed on ego, seeking oneself in God, making him the means of self-discovery. 'Personal' religion, by contrast, is ontological, involving the apprehension of what it is to be a person: it is focussed on fulfilling God's design in Creation rather than on immediate self-discovery.

Such a distinction may be useful in determining our approach towards the Myers-Briggs typology which is currently so influential. This typology, a development from Jungian character-typology, is undoubtedly helpful in freeing the personality for greater responsiveness to spirit. Our understanding of the relationship between self and ego will insure against the potential for idolatry of ego within the system, in its tendency to establish personality as central in spiritual life. Among its practitioners we find, for example, attempts to locate all eight personality types in Jesus and thus to consider his personality as the model for ours. 'Subjective' religion is therefore nurtured, with personality rather than person-hood, as the central concern; Jesus, Saviour and Brother is replaced by Jesus the model for my personality growth. Such is the danger inherent in the system, a danger averted by a grasp of the concept of selfhood and of the subjective-personal distinction. Firmly adhered to, this concept enables us to use the typology as a tool while eschewing it as a total spiritual path.

[1] Fr. Lev. Gillet, *Orthodox Spirituality* (S.P.C.K., London, 2nd ed. 1978) p.23.

This concept is also vital in approaching that other popular personality system, the Enneagram. The Enneagram presupposes an innocent self which becomes distorted and fixated by social pressures into one of nine compulsive survival-strategies; in its terminology the 'ego.' Growth is a question of 'redeeming' the compulsion, so to enable free 'surrendering to our essence', and the discovery of true selfhood.

Superficially similar in terminology, this system is far from the Christian concept of selfhood, for it operates totally within the personality. The self is 'the focus of one's inner resources and strengths': rather than to a capacity for God through receptiveness of spirit to Spirit, this refers to the potential of the personality. The centre for self is found within the individual, whereas the Christian understanding is of that centre lying in God. Likewise, the 'ego' redeemed from its compulsions surrenders, not to a Being beyond itself, but to its own essence, to the fuller personality of which it has been unaware.

This system promotes a bigger, less inhibited personality which may, consequently, be more receptive to spirit. However, since those who use the typology tend to assert that its purpose is the liberation of the self, the possibility of idolatry of ego is evident. Knowledge of the full Christian vision of selfhood will enable the use of insights gained from this sytem while firmly opposing the view of reality it propounds.[1]

This vision of the self also offers considerable help in our social and ethical thinking, for it overcomes the individual/society conflict and revises our notion of duty. Too often we have understood 'duty' as a set of externally imposed obligations whereas, viewed ontologically, it is what is owed another by virtue of what they, and we, are. It arises from within our spiritual nature. We have a 'duty' to love one another, not as an externally enforced commandment but because we are made in the image of a God who is Love. It is our 'duty' to care for the rights of others, not as a result simply of some political conviction but because we must be true to our nature as brothers and sisters. In the words of the Cambridge Platonists we must 'exercise our naturals'.[2] This understanding of duty may radically alter our approach to problems of relationships, both domestic and societal: it could alter, too, the way we educate our feelings about the demands of being social creatures.

On the larger social scale this vision of the self as son and daughter enables the development of a critique of political and social matters which is thoroughly theological, independent of any political ideology. From this understanding of the human person it is possible to deduce a concept of structural sin, for example: there is no need to look towards a Marxist analysis of society, with the inevitable subtle secularization of viewpoint which ensues. Churchmen will inevitably prove more formidable critics if they cannot be dismissed as meddlers in politics, while their rootedness in the belief in brotherhood would enable them to offer an alternative to the conflict-models dominating political thought and action.

[1] A useful summary of these two typologies and of the assumptions of its proponents is found in Betty Smyth r.c. 'Personality inventories', in *The Vision* (Journal of the National Retreat Centre, 1988) pp.5-6.
[2] de Pauley, *op. cit.* p.62.

Returning to the domestic concerns of the Church this vision of selfhood and relationship may cause some questioning of our attitudes to worship and community life. At the moment the concern in all Churches seems to be the affirmation of the communal nature of worship. More often than not this results in an over-emphasis upon the horizontal, i.e. the audibly and visibly expressed relationship between members of a congregation, at the expense of the vertical i.e. the expression of relationship to God. We are caught in 'either-or' thinking, envisaging the choice as between individual-istic reverence towards God or corporate response to God in one another, manifested by 'chumminess' rather than by reverence. If we understand, however, that the bonds between us are not of our making, that they exist in the depths of our being and are consubstantial, as it were, with our bond with God, the conflict disappears. As a body we can *be* together, in worship of the One-in-Three who gives us our uniqueness and our unity. We are freed to develop a more contemplative approach to liturgy, to discover that participation is not identical with maximum physical activity, to experience and show the reverence that is owed to the holiness of our neighbour. As Thomas Carlyle frequently said, we should take off our shoes before our neighbour, for he is the Temple of the Shekinah, the dwelling for the glory of God. Can we truthfully claim that this sense of the mystery of God in the human person characterizes our liturgies or our life together as Christians?

Furthermore, where this sense of the ontological unity of persons existed there would be a shift in our concept of community. We would see our activity as removing obstacles to its revelation rather than as itself creating community. We would not regard as 'active' members only those with the time, energy or inclination to support 'Church efforts'. We would not fall into the trap of taking as our model the social club or the care group in which visible active involvement is the main criterion for assessing mem-bership and commitment. At present we are all conscious of loneliness as the great modern disease, loneliness that arises in part from the individualism which has attacked our recognition of mutual belonging. The great danger for our churches lies in attempting to cure the disease through social organization while still maintaining in its approach and teaching the individualistic model of Man from which it springs.

The concept of selfhood outlined here is radically opposed to the secularization which is now deeply engrained in our churches,[1] and it offers us one weapon in opposing it. If we embrace it we will never again be able to say easily 'be yourself', but when we do so we will know what we mean, what hope of glory we are offering. With this vision we will be able to offer pastoral care and social action which both honours our 'immortal longings' and accepts our frailty, and which transcends our customary conflicts between self and others, individual freedom and social responsibility. It will enable us to see sacrifice, in whatever way it enters our life, as integral to, rather than destructive of, our selfhood. It will enable us to see God present in our experiences of diminution, not as the repair-man intervening from outside, but as the meaning of those experiences. And it will give us the task of communicating this apprehension of glory to the world:

'The glory of God is a living man;
and the glory of Man is the vision of God.'[2]

[1] See the interesting review article of *The Study of Spirituality* by Norman Russell in *Sobor-nost* 9, 1, (1988), 72-75.
[2] Bettenson, *op. cit.*